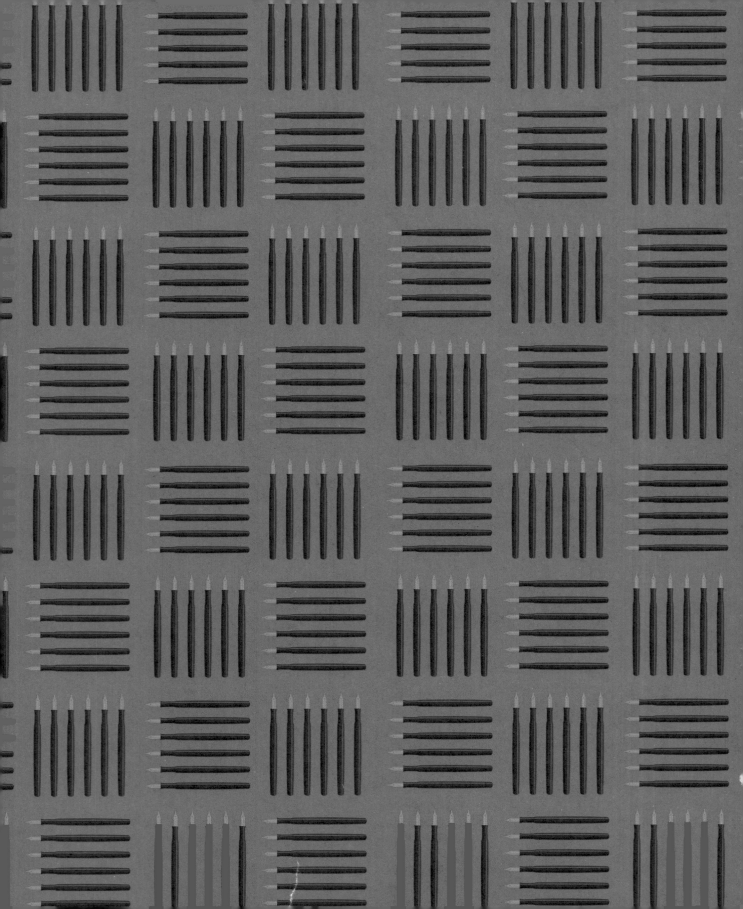

ANNE FRANK

GREAT LIVES IN GRAPHICS

Button
BOOKS

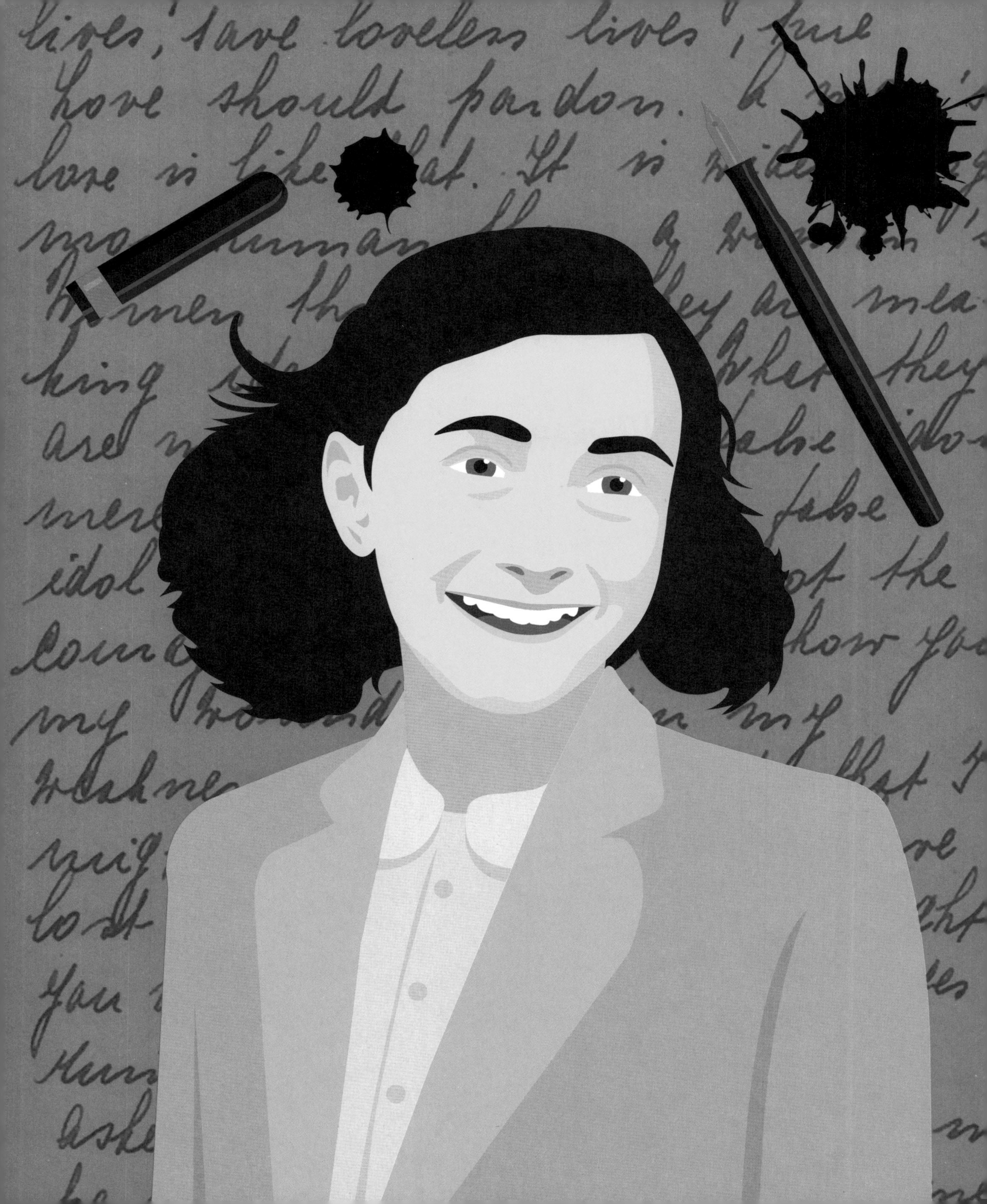
lives, save loveless lives", true
love should pardon.

Anne Frank is one of the most famous writers in the world. She had only just turned 13 when she and her Jewish family were forced to go into hiding from the Nazis during World War II. Afraid that they would be discovered at any moment, they spent more than two years living in cramped, secret rooms above her father's workplace in Amsterdam. Each day she wrote in her diary, sometimes about everyday events, sometimes about her thoughts and feelings. She loved to write and dreamed of becoming a famous author when the war was over.

Sadly, her father Otto was the only member of her family to survive, but Anne's diary lives on – it was saved and published a few years later, turning her dream into a reality. Today it has sold over 30 million copies and has been translated into more than 70 languages. Her words paint a vivid picture of what life was like for a young Jewish girl growing up during such a terrible time in history. And her diary is an important reminder of the dangers of hatred and prejudice.

ANNE'S WORLD

1929
Anne is born on 12 June in Frankfurt, Germany

1930
Clarence Birdseye invents frozen food
· · · · · · · · · · · · · · ·
Pluto is discovered as the ninth planet

1931
Empire State Building opens in New York

1932
Amelia Earhart is first woman to fly solo across the Atlantic

1933
Adolf Hitler becomes leader of Germany
· · · · · · · · · · · · · · ·
The Frank family move to Amsterdam

1934
Anne goes to a Dutch school

1936
Jesse Owens wins four golds at the Berlin Olympics

1938
The Germans begin rounding up Jews

1939
Germany invades Poland. Britain and France declare war on Germany

1940
Germany invades the Netherlands
. . . .
Anne and her sister Margot go to a separate Jewish school

1941
Japan bombs Pearl Harbor. America and Canada join the war

1942
Anne's dad gives her a diary for her 13th birthday
. . . .
The Frank family go into hiding
. . . .
Fritz Pfeffer joins the family in hiding

1944
D-Day: Allied troops land in France
. . . .
The Gestapo discover the hideaways

1945
Anne's mother Edith dies, her dad Otto is freed
. . . .
Anne and Margot die in Bergen-Belsen camp
. . . .
Germany surrenders and war in Europe ends
. . . .
Otto returns to Amsterdam
. . . .
Helper Miep gives Anne's diary to Otto

1943
The war is changing – the Allies are making progress

1947
Anne's diary is published

ANNE FRANK
Het Achter-huis
DAGBOEKBRIEVEN
VAN 14 JUNI 1942 - 1 AUGUSTUS 1944

ALL ABOUT ANNE

If you could whizz back in time to meet Anne, chances are you wouldn't get a word in edgeways because she was quite a chatterbox. At school in Amsterdam she was often caught talking when she shouldn't be and given an essay as punishment, with titles like: *"A Chatterbox"*, *"An Incorrigible Chatterbox"*, and *"Quack, Quack, Quack Said Miss Chatterback"*. Curious and outspoken, Anne was popular and often the ringleader. If they'd had bullet journals in those days, here's what hers may have looked like . . .

I.D. INFORMATION

FULL NAME: ANNELIES MARIE FRANK

NICKNAME: ANNE, OR "CLOWN ANNE" (BECAUSE I LIKE TO MAKE MY FRIENDS LAUGH)

BIRTHDAY: 12 JUNE, 1929

STAR SIGN: GEMINI

RELIGION: JEWISH

EYE COLOUR: BROWN

HAIR COLOUR: BROWN

FAVOURITE COLOUR: GREEN

PET: CAT MOORTJE

> "Will I ever be able to write something great, will I ever become a journalist or a writer? I hope so, oh, I hope so very much because writing allows me to record everything, all my thoughts, ideas and fantasies"
>
> Anne Frank, diary entry 5 April, 1944 (15 years old)

I LOVE:
GAMES, SKATING, READING, MOVIE STARS

BFFS:
LUCIE, SANNE, HANNELI, JUULTJE, KITTY, MARY, LETJE, MARTHA

MY FAVOURITE SUBJECTS:
HISTORY, ART

I DON'T LIKE:
MATHS

DREAM JOB:
JOURNALIST, FAMOUS WRITER

DID YOU KNOW?

Anne dreamed of travelling to Paris and London. She wanted to study the history of art while seeing "beautiful dresses" and "doing all kind of exciting things"

ON MY WISH LIST:

- LIPSTICK
- EYEBROW PENCIL
- BATH SALTS
- BATH POWDER
- EAU-DE-COLOGNE
- SOAP
- POWDER PUFF

FIRST KISS:
PETER VAN PELS

SOAP

NEW RULES

Achtung!

NAZI DEMAND No.1

FROM NOW ON WHENEVER YOU GO OUTSIDE YOU MUST WEAR A YELLOW STAR BADGE PRINTED WITH "JUDE", THE GERMAN WORD FOR JEW. THIS IS SO WE KNOW YOU'RE DIFFERENT FROM OTHER PEOPLE

ACHTUNG!

NAZI DEMAND No.2

You must hand over your bicycle if you have one, and you are banned from riding in a car, even your own. You're not allowed to use trams, either

Achtung!

NAZI DEMAND No.3

You must not go shopping between the hours of 3pm and 5pm

DID YOU KNOW? The Nazis were anti-Semitic. This means they didn't like Jewish people

Anne and her family were German Jews and World War II was a terrible time for Jewish people. Germany's leader, Adolf Hitler, gave lots of speeches to big crowds saying the Jews were to blame for the country's problems. Some people believed his ideas. Those who followed him were called Nazis, and they punished anyone who didn't agree with them. Before long, Hitler had become a powerful dictator and he made up a new set of unfair rules just for Jews that made their lives very difficult. You can read them below. Can you imagine being told that you and your family had to follow these but most people in your country didn't?

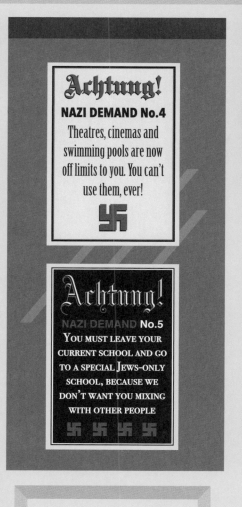

Achtung!

NAZI DEMAND No.4

Theatres, cinemas and swimming pools are now off limits to you. You can't use them, ever!

Achtung!

NAZI DEMAND No.5

YOU MUST LEAVE YOUR CURRENT SCHOOL AND GO TO A SPECIAL JEWS-ONLY SCHOOL, BECAUSE WE DON'T WANT YOU MIXING WITH OTHER PEOPLE

Achtung!

NAZI DEMAND No.6

YOU ARE NOT ALLOWED TO LEAVE YOUR HOUSE BETWEEN THE HOURS OF 8PM AND 6AM, EVEN TO GO INTO YOUR OWN GARDEN

Achtung!

NAZI DEMAND No.7

You must give up all outdoor sports, these are now forbidden

The Nazis chose the swastika as their symbol. In the ancient Indian language of Sanskrit, swastika means "wellbeing". The symbol had been seen as a positive sign for thousands of years before the Nazis used it on their flags, badges and armbands to make people feel afraid of them

NEUTRAL COUNTRIES

ALLIED COUNTRIES

AXIS-CONTROLLED COUNTRIES

AXIS COUNTRIES

64 MILLION
people died in World War II. That's almost the same as the entire population of Great Britain

The Franks arrive in the Netherlands in 1934

IRELAND

UNITED KINGDOM

NETHERLANDS

AMSTERDAM

BELGIUM

WAR OF THE WORLD

FRANCE

Adolf Hitler wanted Germany to grow and become more powerful. On 1 September, 1939, Germany invaded Poland and World War II began. Hitler joined forces with Italy and Japan and together they were known as the **Axis** powers. They fought against the **Allied** powers of Britain, France, the Soviet Union, China and the United States.

"The victor will never be asked if he told the truth"

PORTUGAL

SPAIN

NORWAY

SWEDEN

DENMARK

Anne is born in Frankfurt in 1929

DID YOU KNOW?

The United States didn't join the war until 1941, when Japan attacked Pearl Harbor

SOVIET UNION

FRANKFURT

GERMANY

POLAND

BERGEN-BELSEN

CZECHOSLOVAKIA

Anne and her sister Margot catch typhus and die in Bergen-Belsen concentration camp

AUSTRIA

HUNGARY

ROMANIA

SWITZERLAND

YUGOSLAVIA

BULGARIA

ITALY

ALBANIA

TURKEY

GREECE

ESCAPE TO AMSTERDAM

DID YOU KNOW?

When Anne got to Amsterdam she had to learn to speak **DUTCH!**

When Anne was just four years old the Frank family fled to Amsterdam in the Netherlands. Hitler had become leader of Germany and started to persecute the Jews and Anne's father Otto felt worried for their safety. When people have to leave their home to escape danger, they are called refugees.

HOW MANY REFUGEES WERE THERE?

Around

60 MILLION

Europeans became refugees during World War II

WHY DIDN'T THEY LEAVE EUROPE?

The Frank family tried to escape to America, but the US government and the public only wanted to accept a certain number of Jewish refugees for three main reasons:

RACIAL DISCRIMINATION

They felt afraid of people who were different to them

SECURITY

They worried some of them might be Nazi spies

THE ECONOMY

They didn't think there'd be enough jobs for everyone

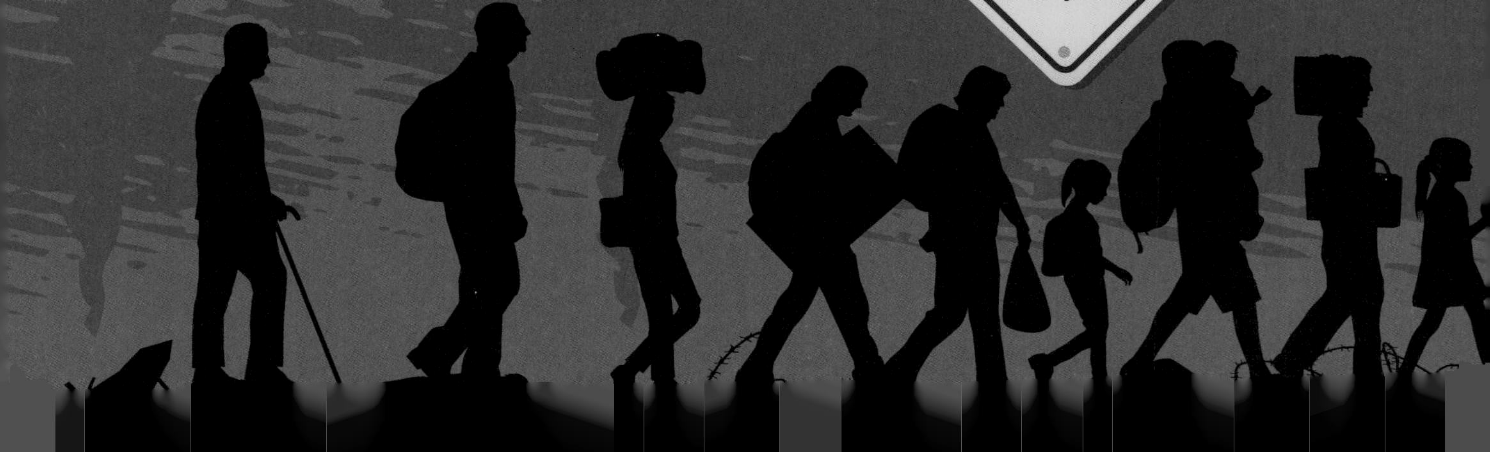

ARE THERE REFUGEES TODAY?

Yes. Today we are in the middle of another refugee crisis. Millions of people are fleeing from war and violence in countries like Syria, Iraq and Afghanistan

TURKEY

SYRIA

IRAQ

JORDAN

IRAN

AFGHANISTAN

PAKISTAN

SAUDI ARABIA

OMAN

HOW DO THEY TRAVEL?

Often refugees have to travel a long way by car, lorry, boat and foot

WHAT PROBLEMS DO THEY FACE?

Refugees can struggle to:
- Find shelter
- Find food and water
- Feel safe

"I think that all the German Jews are searching the world today and there is no room for them anymore"

Written by Anne's mother, Edith Frank, in a letter to a friend in 1937

THE SECRET ANNEX

When Anne was almost 11, Germany invaded the Netherlands. This meant that the Franks were in danger all over again. Anne and her older sister Margot were forced to leave their Dutch school and go to a Jews-only one. The Frank family, afraid they would be arrested by the Nazi police, went into hiding in secret rooms above her father's workplace at Prinsengracht 263.

FULL HOUSE

A week after the Franks went into hiding, another Jewish family joined them – Hermann and Auguste van Pels, and their teenage son Peter. Last to arrive was a dentist called Fritz Pfeffer

Anne's dad Otto spent months getting the secret rooms above his factory ready in case they would need to hide from the Nazis. Anne called it the "secret annex"

FALSE TRAIL

Anne didn't know they might go into hiding until they had to. They left their home in a mess so that the Nazis would think they'd left suddenly.

Because Jews weren't allowed on buses, they had to walk several kilometres from their apartment to her dad's workplace.

They wore their clothes in lots of layers so that they wouldn't be seen carrying suitcases

The only way to get into the annex was through a secret doorway hidden behind a specially built bookcase

1 SECOND FLOOR ABOVE STREET LEVEL

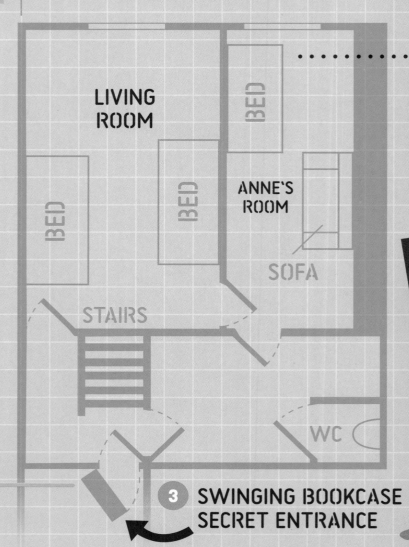

LIVING ROOM

BED

BED

ANNE'S ROOM

BED

SOFA

STAIRS

WC

3 SWINGING BOOKCASE SECRET ENTRANCE

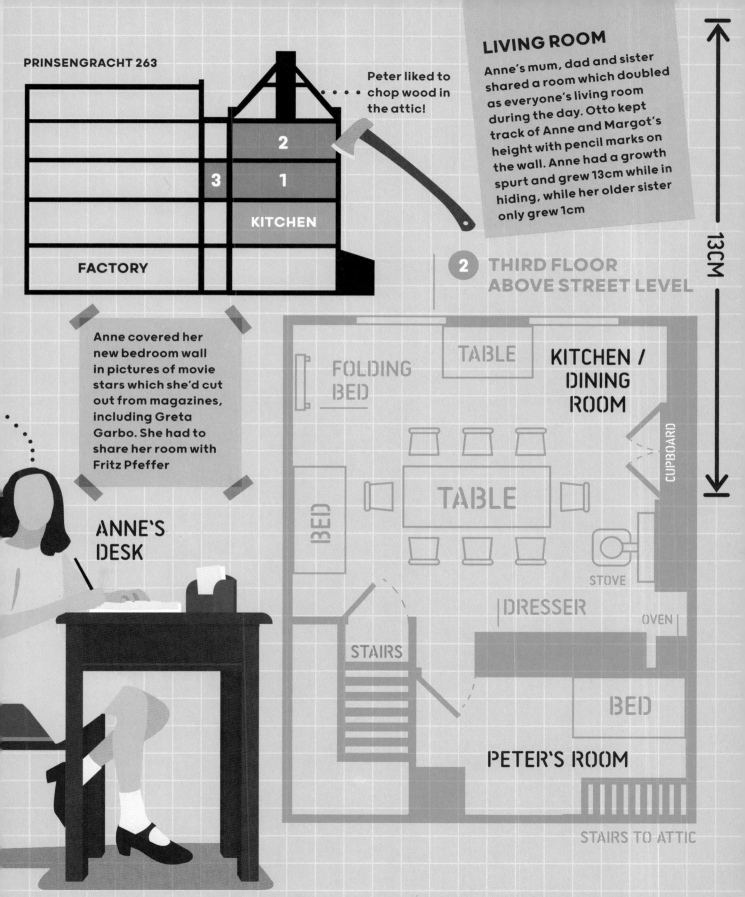

PRINSENGRACHT 263

2

3 **1**

KITCHEN

FACTORY

Peter liked to •••• chop wood in the attic!

LIVING ROOM

Anne's mum, dad and sister shared a room which doubled as everyone's living room during the day. Otto kept track of Anne and Margot's height with pencil marks on the wall. Anne had a growth spurt and grew 13cm while in hiding, while her older sister only grew 1cm

13CM

2 **THIRD FLOOR ABOVE STREET LEVEL**

Anne covered her new bedroom wall in pictures of movie stars which she'd cut out from magazines, including Greta Garbo. She had to share her room with Fritz Pfeffer

ANNE'S DESK

FOLDING BED

TABLE

TABLE

KITCHEN / DINING ROOM

CUPBOARD

BED

STOVE

DRESSER

OVEN

STAIRS

BED

PETER'S ROOM

STAIRS TO ATTIC

Dear Kitty...

On Anne's 13th birthday, just a few weeks before they went into hiding, her father gave her a present – a red-and-white checked notebook that she had seen in a local shop.

Anne wrote her diary in Dutch

Lieve Kitty,

Over the next two years, Anne wrote faithfully in her diary. She pretended she was writing letters to imaginary friends, and her favourite of these was Kitty.

"Dear Kitty... I like writing to you most, you know that don't you, and I hope the feeling is mutual."

22 September, 1942

Living in such cramped conditions, the group had its ups and downs.

"You only really get to know people when you've had a jolly good row with them. Then and only then can you judge their true characters!"

28 September, 1942

Anne chose to use the notebook as a diary and began writing in it straight away.

"I hope I will be able to confide everything to you, as I have never been able to confide in anyone, and I hope you will be a great source of comfort and support."

12 June, 1942

Living in the annex, Anne often felt scared. When a workman came to fill the fire extinguishers in the warehouse below, they were terrified their hiding place had been discovered.

"My hand still shakes, although it's two hours since we had the shock."

20 October, 1942

Despite the hardships, Anne realised they were lucky to be alive.

"If I just think of how we live here, I usually come to the conclusion that it is a paradise compared with how other Jews who are not in hiding must be living."

1 May, 1943

Anne wrote this over 70 years ago but it stands just as true today, don't you think?

"People can tell you to keep your mouth shut, but it doesn't stop you having your own opinion. Even if people are still very young, they shouldn't be prevented from saying what they think."

2 March, 1944

Anne wrote two versions of her diary. One day she heard a call on the radio for people to save their war-time diaries as historical records of the suffering that occurred under Nazi occupation. When Anne heard this she began writing a new version of her diary, ready to be published once the war was over

Being cooped up in the annex, unable to go outside, was hard for Anne.

"I believe that if I live here any longer, I'll turn into a dried-up old beanstalk and all I really want is to be an honest-to-goodness teenager!"

15 January, 1944

Anne's writing was often wise beyond her years.

"What is done cannot be undone, but one can prevent it happening again."

7 May, 1944

Optimism was one of Anne's most important strengths.

"At such moments I don't think about all the misery, but about the beauty that still remains."

7 March, 1944

Anne used a fountain pen with grey-blue ink to write in her diary. Some people think parts were written in ballpoint pen and that this means the diary is a fake, but experts analysed the book and confirmed no ballpoint pen was ever used

THE HIDERS

In total, eight people hid in the secret annex at Prinsengracht 263. So who were they and what did Anne think about them?

EDITH FRANK AKA NORA ROBIN

Anne's mum did her best to make meals for everyone from the limited food supplies. As they were stuck together for hours each day, Anne fell out with her regularly, saying: "I usually keep my mouth shut when I'm irritated and she does too, and that makes things seem to go better."

OTTO FRANK AKA FREDERICK ROBIN

Anne's dad continued with his business affairs and helped Anne with her studies. She loved her father very much, saying: "Daddy's a sweetheart; he may get mad at me, but it never lasts longer than five minutes."

AKA...
NAME SWAP!

When Anne rewrote her diaries for publication she created pseudonyms (made-up names) for everyone living in the annex

DID YOU KNOW?

Anne wasn't that fond of Fritz Pfeffer, and the name she gave him – Dussel – translates as "idiot" in German!

MARGOT FRANK AKA BETTY ROBIN

Three years older than Anne, Margot was quieter and more sensible than her lively sister. Anne described her as "naturally good, kind and clever, perfection itself, but I seem to have enough mischief for the two of us".

ANNE FRANK AKA ANNE ROBIN

When Anne reached the hiding place she wrote in her diary about having to pack in a hurry: "The first thing I put in was this diary, then hair curlers, handkerchiefs, schoolbooks, a comb, old letters; I put in the craziest things with the idea that we were going into hiding. But I'm not sorry, memories mean more to me than dresses."

HERMANN VAN PELS AKA MR VAN DAAN

Hermann worked with Otto and helped set up their hiding place. He knew a butcher he could trust who supplied the hiders with sausages and meat whenever he could. Hermann was the joker in the secret house, but when he was in a bad mood, Anne wasn't his biggest fan.

AUGUSTE VAN PELS AKA PETRONELLA VAN DAAN

Anne described Auguste as the "busy housewife". Auguste had a big fight with Hermann after he forced her to sell her favourite fur coat when they ran out of money. But they never stayed mad for long and had pet names for each other: "Putti" for Hermann and "Kerli" for Auguste.

PETER VAN PELS AKA PETER VAN DAAN

Anne wasn't impressed with 15-year-old Peter when he first arrived. "Peter's going on 16," she wrote. "A shy, awkward boy whose company won't amount to much." But the longer they were in hiding, the closer they became, and soon they fell in love.

FRITZ PFEFFER AKA ALBERT DUSSEL

The dentist and friend of the Frank family was the last housemate to arrive. Anne wasn't happy that they were in the same room, especially as he didn't like to share their little table.

THE WISHING TREE

From the attic window, Anne could glimpse a majestic horse chestnut tree. Living in constant fear of bomb blasts and discovery, she would look at the tree and escape for a brief moment. In her diary, she wrote: "From my favourite spot on the floor I look up at the blue sky and the bare chestnut tree, on whose branches little raindrops glisten like silver, and at the seagulls and other birds as they glide on the wind."

IS THE TREE STILL STANDING TODAY?

No, sadly – it was over 160 years old when it was destroyed during a storm in 2010. But there's a happy ending to this story because 11 saplings were taken from the ancient tree and planted around the world in memory of Anne and those who died during the Holocaust.

THE HELPERS

These kind and brave people risked everything to bring food and supplies to the hiders. They also brought news of the outside world and helped keep up the spirits of Anne and her housemates.

VICTOR KUGLER AKA MR KRALER

Victor worked with Otto in the factory. He came up with the clever idea of creating a revolving bookcase to hide the entrance to the secret house. After the war, when he was asked why he risked his life to help the people hiding in the annex, he replied: "I had to help them; they were my friends."

MIEP & JAN GIES AKA MIEP & HENK VAN SANTEN

Miep worked in the office below the annex and helped by bringing meat and vegetables for those in hiding. She managed to sneak in the odd library book, too. When the hiding place was discovered by the Nazi police, Miep found Anne's diaries and papers and kept them, hoping one day to return to them Anne.

SECRET ENTRANCE!

JOHANNES KLEIMAN AKA MR KOOPHUIS

Johannes was a good friend to Otto and helped to keep his businesses running. It was Johannes who suggested to Otto that they create a hiding place above the warehouse. And he was the first point of contact for the hiders – he helped them send letters to family abroad and dealt with problems in the annex. The stress of the secret he was hiding took its toll, though, and he suffered greatly with stomach problems.

JOHAN & BEP VOSKUIJL AKA MR VOSSEN & ELLI VOSSEN

Bep brought the hiders bread and milk and, as the youngest of the helpers, she was a good friend to Anne. Anne even managed to convince her to spend a night in the annex, but Bep was too scared to sleep: "To tell you the truth, I was terrified. Every time I heard a tree creaking in the October wind or a car driving along the canal, I grew afraid. I was grateful when morning came, and I was able to get back to work."

YUCK!

During the war, people were put on "rations", which meant only certain types of food – and small amounts – were available. As time went on it became harder for the helpers to find food, so the housemates were hungry most of the time. Poor Anne would also have had to eat foods that she really didn't like

- Brown beans
- Potato kugel (made from potatoes, onion, flour and eggs, if they were available)
- Turnip greens
- Rotten carrots
- Dumplings (made from flour, yeast and water)
- As a treat, jam on unbuttered bread

"We, who fill our stomachs with nothing but boiled lettuce, raw lettuce, spinach, spinach and more spinach. Maybe we'll end up being as strong as Popeye, though so far I've seen no sign of it!"

A DAY IN THE LIFE

Can you imagine being stuck inside cramped rooms, not allowed to even open a window, for more than two years? What would you do to fight the boredom? Here's what an average day in the annex was like for Anne.

9pm

Start preparing for bed. The shared living spaces are turned back into bedrooms. People take their turn in the bathroom and Anne puts the blackout screens back up

7:30-9pm

Peter fetches the bread that has been left for them in the office downstairs. Otto types business letters on the typewriter. Anne and Margot do chores (there's no escaping them, even in hiding!). Sometimes they listen to music and news on the radio

7pm DINNER
Anne's mum Edith cooks dinner with Auguste

5:45pm
The factory workers go home, so everyone is free to move around the building

1:45-5:30pm
Anne records her innermost thoughts and feelings in her diary. Sometimes she plays Quinta, a favourite board game, with Margot. The adults often have an afternoon nap

12:30pm LUNCH

The workers down below go home for a break. While the coast is clear, the "helpers" come upstairs with rations and bread. Miep stays in the office to keep an eye on things. It's finally safe to make some noise, so the radio is tuned in to BBC News to find out what is going on in the outside world

23 22 21 20 19 18 17 16 15 14 13

DID YOU KNOW?

Anne spent

761

days in the secret annex

FUNNY GIRL

Anne tried to see the funny side of things to keep her spirits up. When Fritz Pfeffer arrived, she wrote out a *Prospectus and Guide to the Secret Annex*, pretending it was a sort of boarding house. She described it as "Open all year round", with "cosy wood stoves for heating" and called the diet "low fat"

ANNE HATED SUNDAYS!

In her diary, she wrote:
"I wander from one room to the next, down the stairs and back up again and feel like a songbird that has had its wings torn off and flies against the bars of its cage in total darkness. I lie down on a divan and sleep in order to shorten the time, the silence."

6:45am

Alarm clock goes off in the Van Pels' bedroom. The kettle is put on and everyone takes their turn in the bathroom. Anne's first job of the day? To remove the blackout screens from the windows

8:30-9am

This is a dangerous time for the hideaways because the warehouse workers have started their day and are able to hear any noise from above

9am BREAKFAST

At the beginning of the stay in the house this would have been bread and jam, or some of the tinned food that Otto had stashed before they moved in

9:30am

Anne and Margot spend the morning studying while the others read or start to get lunch ready

✗ YOU CAN'T...

Go outside

Flush the toilet during the daytime

Open the curtains during the daytime

"I long so much for him to kiss me, but that kiss is taking its own sweet time. Does he still think of me as a friend? Don't I mean anything more?"

First impressions

"A shy, awkward boy going on 16, whose company won't amount to much."

First kiss

"Isn't it an important day for every girl when she gets her first kiss? I can't tell you, Kitty, the feeling that ran through me. I was too happy for words, and I think he was too."

QUIET

SWEET

SENSITIVE

It was definitely not love at first sight when Anne and Peter met on 13 July, 1942. But after spending so many months together, the young teenagers began to fall in love. They would snatch precious moments in the attic together, away from the others. Anne recorded this exciting time in her diary, along with some of her doubts about their relationship.

Anne *Loves* Peter

PETER VAN PELS

Born:	8 November, 1926
Birthplace:	Osnabrück, Germany
Height:	5ft 7in (1.7m)
Star sign:	Scorpio

Things in common
Mums who annoy us!

Relationship doubts
"If I were older and he wanted to marry me, what would my answer be? Anne, be honest! You wouldn't be able to marry him. But it's so hard to let go. Peter still has too little character, too little willpower, too little courage and strength. Oh, it's so hard, the eternal struggle between heart and mind."

Racy moment
"At eight-thirty, I stood up and went to the window, where we always say goodbye. He came over to me, and I threw my arms round his neck and kissed him on his left cheek. I was about to kiss the other cheek when my mouth met his, and we pressed our lips together. In a daze, we embraced, over and over again, never to stop, oh!"

Favourite memory
"What could be nicer than sitting before an open window, enjoying nature, listening to the birds sing, feeling the sun on your cheeks and holding a darling boy in your arms?"

SIGNS YOU'RE FALLING
in love...

Pupils get larger

Faster heart rate

Butterflies in the tummy

Wobbly knees

Did you know?
Margot felt a bit jealous of the lovebirds because she wanted someone to share her feelings with too

AGE:	8-80
WHO:	Men, women and children
JOB:	To work secretly against the Nazis ruling their country
LOCATION:	Every occupied country
AKA:	The Underground

DANGER RATING: 10

Often tortured and killed if captured

RESISTANCE FIGHTER

When Germany invaded and took over a country, a few brave people tried to make life difficult for the Nazis. They formed secret groups known as "the resistance".

NAZIS OUT!

WHAT THEY DID

STRIKES AND DEMONSTRATIONS

Hid Jewish people who were being persecuted

KILLED NAZI SOLDIERS

HELPED ALLIED SOLDIERS AND PILOTS TO ESCAPE

GAVE OUT SECRET LEAFLETS THAT SPOKE OUT AGAINST THE NAZIS

FORGED DOCUMENTS

SABOTAGED COMMUNICATIONS CABLES AND RAILWAY LINES

DID YOU KNOW?

Yugoslavian resistance fighters were so successful they managed to take back their country from the Germans

Collected information about the German army for Allied intelligence

In France, resistance fighters lived in forests deep in the countryside to escape detection

Poland's Home Army was one of the largest resistance groups. It boasted around:

400,000 fighters

AGE:	16-60
WHO:	Mostly men
JOB:	To spy on people and arrest anyone who didn't like what the Nazis were doing
LOCATION:	Nazi Germany and every occupied country
AKA:	The Secret Police

POWERS:
Above the law. Could arrest anyone they chose to

GESTAPO AGENT

The Gestapo were the Nazis' undercover police. They didn't wear uniforms, so people couldn't tell who they were. This made people afraid to speak out against the Nazis in case they were overheard.

WHAT THEY DID

SPIED ON PEOPLE AND ARRESTED THEM IF THEY HAD DIFFERENT VIEWS TO THE NAZI PARTY

ROUNDED UP JEWS READY FOR DEPORTATION

Blackmailed and tortured the people they arrested

Used informants (regular citizens who weren't Gestapo but agreed with the Nazis) to gather information

MADE PEOPLE AFRAID TO SPEAK OUT AGAINST THE NAZIS

Helped the German army

TARGETED LEFT-WING POLITICAL GROUPS LIKE THE COMMUNISTS

WORKED TO FIND AND STOP THE RESISTANCE

DID YOU KNOW?

The Gestapo headquarters was on Prinz-Albrecht Street in Berlin, Germany

The Gestapo itself wasn't very big, but it had thousands of informants in Germany and occupied countries who would report anyone who said or did anything against the Nazis

ARRESTED

On Friday 4 August, 1944, the Gestapo raided Prinsengracht 263 and the secret annex was discovered.

10.45am
HANDS UP!

Police officers walk into the factory's front office and point a revolver at Miep, Bep and Johannes, who are working there

11am
THE HUNT BEGINS

The Gestapo officers go into Victor's office and ask him lots of questions. They force him to give them a tour of the building

11:10am
IN THE ANNEX

The hiders have no idea that the Gestapo are in the building. Otto is busy helping Peter with his language lessons

Today we still don't know how the Gestapo found out that Jews were hiding in the secret annex. Some people think they were betrayed by one of the workers in the factory, but this was never proven

12.45pm
DIARY DUMPED

The hiders are told to hand over any valuables. One of the police officers grabs Otto's briefcase, which was holding Anne's diary, and empties it to put the valuables in. Anne's notebooks are scattered across the floor

12.15pm
DISCOVERED!

The police come to the landing with the bookcase, and find the secret entrance. Anne and the other hiders are taken completely by surprise

11:20am
HELPERS WARNED

Jan, Miep's husband, arrives at the front office to have lunch with the hiders. Miep tells him the Gestapo are there and he leaves quickly. Bep is very upset. Johannes tells her to use the phone at a nearby pharmacist to call his wife and let her know what's happened, and then to disappear

1pm
ARRESTED!

Miep hears the Franks, Van Pelses and Pfeffer coming down the stairs. "I could tell from their footsteps that they were coming down like beaten dogs," she would say later. The Gestapo officers bundle Anne and the rest of the hiders into a police van that's waiting outside, along with helpers Johannes and Victor

5pm
DIARY SAVED

When the coast is clear Jan and Bep return to the office to find Miep. The three of them go upstairs to the empty annex and Miep picks up Anne's diaries and papers. She keeps them in a drawer in the office below, hoping one day to return them to Anne

1945
OTTO SURVIVES

Johannes is released two weeks later, and Victor manages to escape while being deported to Germany. But the hiders are not so lucky. They are sent to a concentration camp where Anne and Margot catch typhus and die in March 1945. Otto is the only survivor

*All times are approximate

A dream come true

On 8 May, 1945 Germany surrendered and World War II ended. Otto was the only one of those hiding in the secret annex to survive the Nazi concentration camps. Ten months after his arrest, he returned to Amsterdam. He was relieved to discover that all the helpers had survived the war, and he moved in with Miep and Jan. Miep gave Otto Anne's diary and he was amazed to read all that she had written. Two years later he had it published and Anne's dream of becoming a famous writer was finally fulfilled.

THE DIARY OF ANNE FRANK

Anne wanted to call the diary "Het Acherhuis", which translates as "The Secret Annex", so that was the title of the first Dutch edition

Did you know?

Otto remarried in 1953 and moved to Switzerland. He died in 1980 aged 91

It was first translated from Dutch into German in

1950

Translated into over

70

languages

Next it was translated into English for the UK and USA in

1952

It is now the most translated Dutch book ever

It has sold over

30

million copies

The diary has inspired 100+ books, poems, plays, movies, musical pieces, artworks and dances

5 of the most-read books of all time

MILLIONS OF COPIES SOLD

700
600
500
400
300
200
100
0

3,900 million — THE HOLY BIBLE

400 million — HARRY POTTER

103 million — The Lord of the Rings

43 million — THE TWILIGHT SAGA

30 million — THE DIARY OF ANNE FRANK

Did you know?

In 1983, a school in Alabama, USA, tried to block Anne's diary from schools because it was "a real downer"

The Diary of Anne Frank has about

86,275 words

341 pages

ANNE FRANK HOUSE

The house with the secret annex at Prinsengracht 263 is now a museum

1957 Established with Otto Frank

1.2 million visitors per year

"How proud Anne would have been if she had lived to see this"

Otto Frank

GLOSSARY

ALLIED POWERS
The group of nations headed by Great Britain, France, the Soviet Union, China and the United States who fought against the Axis powers in World War II

ANTI-SEMITISM
A feeling of hatred towards Jewish people

AXIS POWERS
The group of nations headed by Germany, Italy and Japan who fought against the Allied powers in World War II

COMMUNIST
A person who believes that the government should own everything and share it between its citizens

CONCENTRATION CAMP
A place where people are imprisoned, usually under harsh conditions, without trial

GESTAPO
The Nazi's secret police force

HOLOCAUST
A period of history when millions of Jewish people and others were killed because of their beliefs, race or religion

JEW
A person who is a descendant of the ancient Hebrews or whose religion is Judaism

NAZI
A member of the Nazi Party, the political group led by Adolf Hitler that ruled Germany between 1933 and 1945

OCCUPATION
The control of a place or area by a military force

PERSECUTION
To treat people badly because of their religious or political beliefs

PSEUDONYM
A fake name that someone uses instead of a real name

REFUGEE
A person who has been forced to leave their country to escape persecution, war or natural disaster

RESISTANCE
Groups of people who worked secretly against the Nazis during World War II

SECRET ANNEX
The attic apartment where Anne and her family hid from the Nazis during World War II

SWASTIKA
An ancient symbol used as the emblem of the Nazi Party

TYPHUS
An infectious disease spread by lice, fleas or mites

Button Books

First published 2020 by Button Books, an imprint of Guild of Master Craftsman Publications Ltd, Castle Place, 166 High Street, Lewes, East Sussex, BN7 1XU, UK. Copyright in the Work © GMC Publications Ltd, 2020. ISBN 978 1 78708 060 7. Distributed by Publishers Group West in the United States. All rights reserved. No part of this publication may be reproduced, stored in a retrieval system or transmitted in any form or by any means without the prior permission of the publisher and copyright owner. While every effort has been made to obtain permission from the copyright holders for all material used in this book, the publishers will be pleased to hear from anyone who has not been appropriately acknowledged and to make the correction in future reprints. The publishers and authors can accept no legal responsibility for any consequences arising from the application of information, advice or instructions given in this publication. A catalogue record for this book is available from the British Library. Senior Project Editor: Susie Duff. Design: Matt Carr, Jo Chapman. Illustrations: Alex Bailey, Matt Carr, Shutterstock. Colour origination by GMC Reprographics. Printed and bound in China.

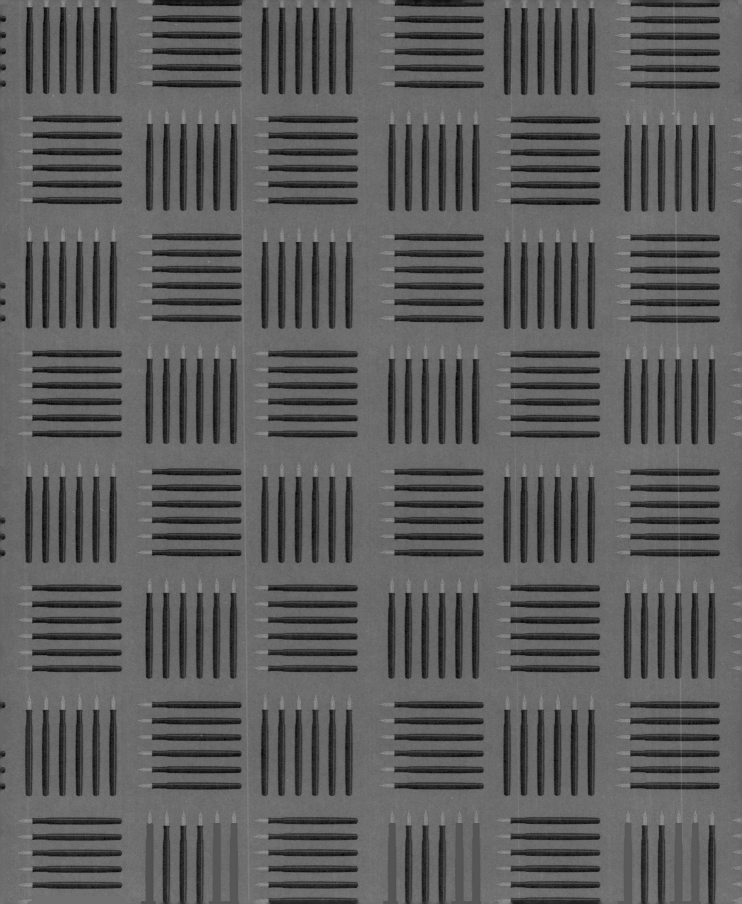

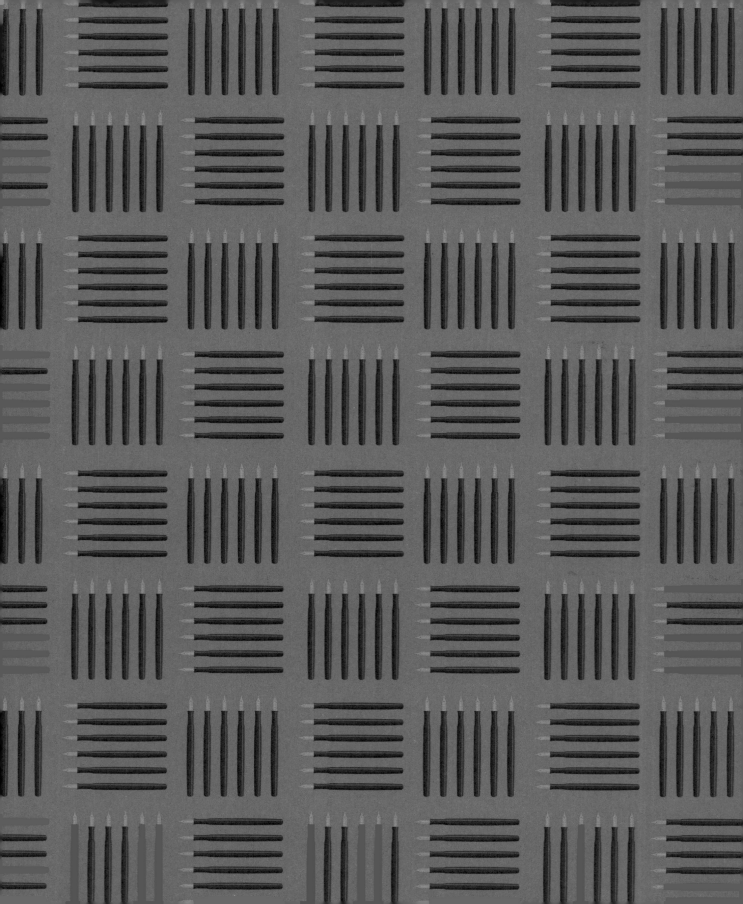